For Michael, Ali, and Georgia
H.M.

To Joan, Mat, Nic, and Katy
P.J.

Text copyright © 1994 by Heather Maisner
Illustrations copyright © 1994 by Peter Joyce

First U.S. edition 1995
First published in Great Britain in 1994 by Walker Books Ltd., London.

Library of Congress Cataloging-in-Publication Data
Maisner, Heather.
The magic hourglass : a time-travel adventure game / Heather Maisner ;
illustrated by Peter Joyce.— 1st U.S. ed.
"First published in Great Britain in 1994 by Walker Books Ltd., London"—T.p. verso.
ISBN 1-56402-446-6
1. Picture puzzles—Juvenile literature.   2. Literary recreations—Juvenile literature.
[1. Geographical recreations.   2. Literary recreations.   3. Picture puzzles.]
I. Joyce, Peter, 1937-   ill. II. Title.
GV1507.P47M35   1995
793.73—dc20   94—10404

2 4 6 8 10 9 7 5 3 1

Printed in Italy

The pictures in this book were done in line and watercolor.

Candlewick Press
2067 Massachusetts Avenue
Cambridge, Massachusetts 02140

THE MAGIC HOURGLASS

A TIME-TRAVEL ADVENTURE GAME

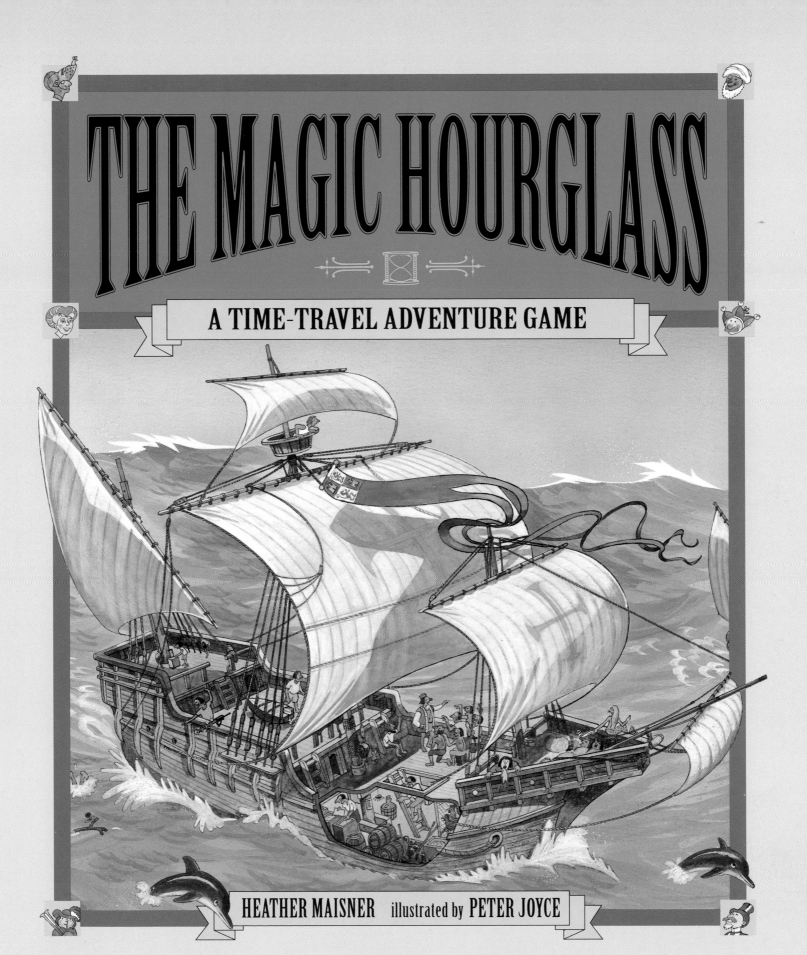

HEATHER MAISNER   illustrated by PETER JOYCE

CANDLEWICK PRESS

CAMBRIDGE, MASSACHUSETTS

TIME CHART

Read the instructions opposite before you start to play.

~ OBJECTS FROM THE PRESENT ~

Do Not Enter sign	telephone pole	television	car
toilet paper roll	office building	electric drill	outboard motor
bicycle	wristwatch	binoculars	electric kettle
toaster	traffic light	lawn mower	camera
radio	desk lamp	motorcycle	traffic cone

Your Great Aunt Fantasia, the famous historian, has sent you this note and a wonderful magic hourglass. Simply touch the hourglass and you will be sent on an amazing journey into the past.

HOW TO BEGIN YOUR JOURNEY

☞ Touch the Magic Hourglass, say "**zoomaway**," and turn the page. Choose Remarkable Moment 1 or Remarkable Moment 2. Read the clues to follow a route through the scene. Discover fascinating facts about the past as you go.

☞ When you have solved the last clue in the scene, look for the Magic Hourglass, now waiting for you and hiding nearby. Be alert! The Magic Hourglass changes color everywhere it goes.

Here are two examples:

☞ When you have found the Magic Hourglass, return to the Time Chart on page 6. Find the hourglass with the same color and turn to the pages numbered beside it. Choose another Remarkable Moment and set off again.

☞ Keep going until the Magic Hourglass turns white again and leads you back to The Present.

☞ Be sure to look out for me wherever you go — I am hiding in four places somewhere in history. And keep a lookout for twenty objects from the present that are lost in the past. They are listed on page 6.

☞ Play with the Magic Hourglass as often as you like. Each game will be different — some long, some short.

Have fun and don't get lost!

Aunt Fantasia

Great Aunt Fantasia

Touch the Magic Hourglass!
Say Zoomaway!

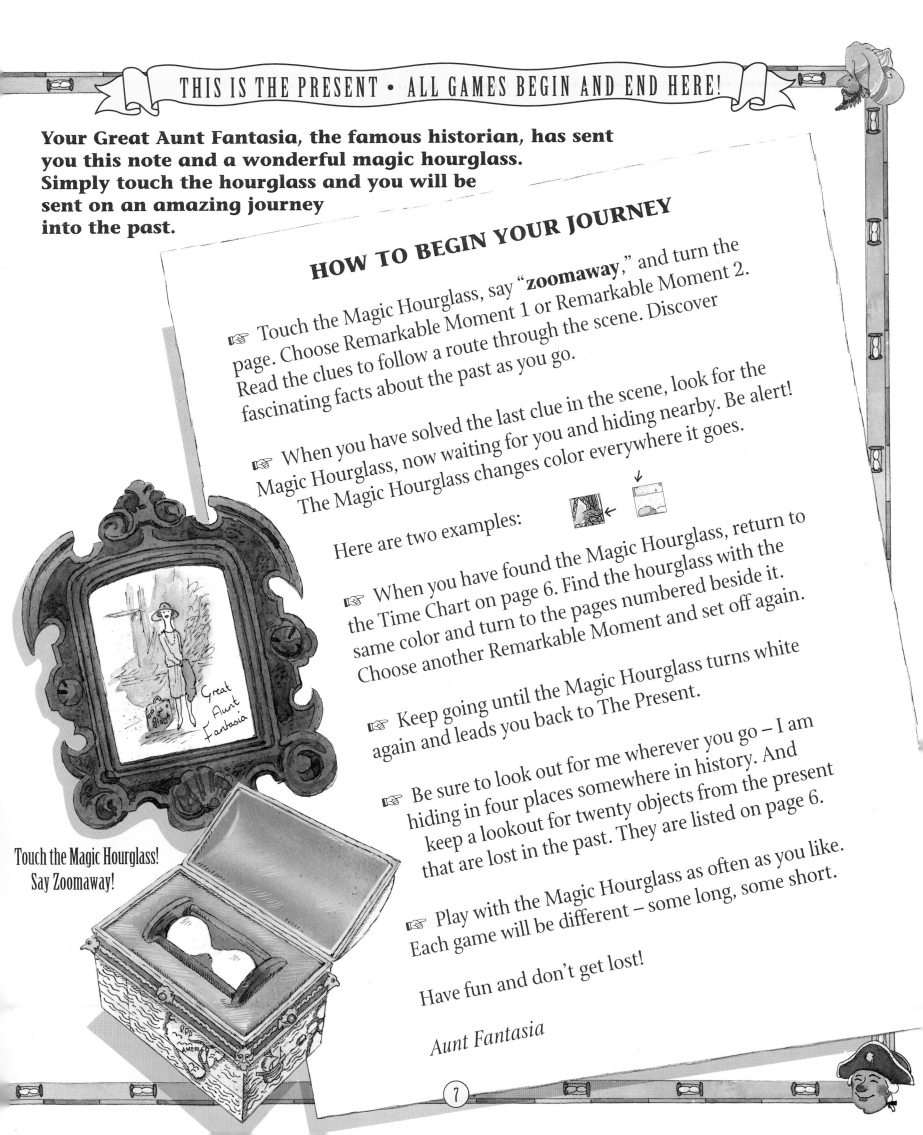

THE WAGON TRAIN GOES WEST

You're in America as the pioneers trek west on the Oregon Trail. They hope to find a better life in green and fertile Oregon, 2,000 miles away. The journey, across prairies, deserts, and mountains, will take four to six months.

~ THE ROUTE ~

☞ Join the last wagon in the line. Families travel together for safety. Wagons are crowded with tools, clothes, linen, and food. You won't see a store for months.

☞ Pass the next wagon and find a runaway iron tire. It's so hot and dry that the wooden wheel has shrunk and the tire has rolled off.

☞ Thirsty? Move on to the circle of wagons where women are washing dishes in leftover cold tea. Ask them for a drink.

☞ Stop by the ox too tired to stand. Many people and animals die on the long journey west.

☞ You're at the river. Cross carefully. When the river is swollen, people can get swept away.

☞ Join the men chasing buffalo. They haven't tasted fresh meat for weeks. Buffalo skins are dried for rawhide and tanned for leather.

☞ Look up at the cliffs on the right. These people sending smoke signals are Plains Indians. There are many tribes with different languages who have lived here for thousands of years.

☞ Ride ahead to the scout, checking the route for dangers. He's a mountain man and has made the western wilderness his home.

☞ **SEEK THE MAGIC HOURGLASS**
   Now it is pale yellow.

AUSTRALIA AT LAST!

It is 1770 and you are with Captain James Cook and his crew, who have just set foot in Australia for the first time. They have come on a scientific voyage from Britain and are exploring the east coast.

THE ROUTE

☞ Find Captain Cook's ship, the *Endeavour*. The crew survived the incredibly long voyage here because he made sure that they ate well and that the ship was kept clean.

☞ Row ashore. Cook calls this Botany Bay, as there are so many fascinating plants growing here.

☞ Hungry? Help the sailors carry two huge stingrays up the beach for lunch.

☞ Now step across to Captain Cook, who is drawing a map. Other explorers have sighted this land before, but Cook is the first to map the east coast.

☞ Cross the beach and meet the two artists. They are drawing plants and animals, because cameras have not yet been invented.

☞ Do you see the man hoisting a flag? Cook is claiming this land for Britain and will call it New South Wales.

☞ Oh dear, someone has fallen into the bushes! It is a scientist collecting plants to take home.

☞ Walk past the kangaroo to meet the aborigines. They have been here for thousands of years. Their religion is called the "Dreamtime." They believe that plants, animals, people, and the landscape are all part of nature. This links them to the land in a very special way.

☞ **SEEK THE MAGIC HOURGLASS**
Now it is green.

PETER THE GREAT

You are in St. Petersburg, Russia. Czar Peter the Great has built his new capital city on marshy swampland in the Gulf of Finland. He wants to modernize Russia and impress the rest of the world. This is Peterhof, his new palace and park.

~ THE ROUTE ~

☞ Start at the palace at the top. Peter planned the park with the help of foreign architects. Soldiers and peasants built it.

☞ Walk down the steps beside the fountains and along the main canal as far as the rabbit.

☞ Lend a hand to two foreign ambassadors digging the garden. Peter makes his guests work hard. Then he invites them to a banquet.

☞ Walk on to the Adam fountain. Peter also plans to build trick fountains that will spurt water at you.

☞ Go toward the sea and join Peter at his desk. Be as quiet as possible. Peter is editing Russia's first newspaper. He's also a carpenter and shipbuilder.

☞ Walk along the shore behind the peasant. He is carrying dirt in his clothes because there are no wheelbarrows. Many peasants have died building St. Petersburg.

☞ Lend your jacket to the noblewoman shivering by the sea. She has had to leave the comfort of her home in Moscow for this cold city that is often flooded.

☞ Follow the dogs and meet the nobleman with a beard. Peter makes all noblemen shave or pay a heavy tax. The man's medallion shows that he has paid the tax.

☞ Stop and talk to Catherine, holding a parasol. She is Peter's second wife. Before she married him she was a peasant. Now he has made her Empress.

☞ **SEEK THE MAGIC HOURGLASS**
Now it is pale yellow.

A RICH AND BUSY CITY

You are in Amsterdam. This city is growing richer every day from fishing, shipping, banking, and trade with the rest of the world.

～ THE ROUTE ～

☞ Find two merchants taking bags of money to the new Bank of Amsterdam.

☞ Follow the black cat across the bridge over the canal. Canals have been built to drain the marshy land so that merchants can build more houses.

☞ Turn and meet the artist by the canal. He's Rembrandt van Rijn, the great Dutch painter. Today he's painting a portrait.

☞ Cross the nearest bridge and join the man looking through a telescope. Telescopes have recently been invented by a Dutch spectacle-maker, who calls them "lookers."

☞ Walk along the canal bank, past the horse and the boat to the man deep in thought. He's a foreign philosopher who can publish ideas here that are not liked in his own country.

☞ Cross the next bridge and run past the cheese seller with the wheelbarrow in front of the new Town Hall. 13,659 long wooden stakes have been driven into the marshy soil to support this building.

☞ Stop and look through the latest Dutch microscope. See germs for the very first time.

☞ Join the man with a map of the world. He is Abel Janszoon Tasman, a Dutch explorer and the first European to have reached New Zealand.

☞ **SEEK THE MAGIC HOURGLASS**
Now it is green.

LAND OF THE SAMURAI

You have arrived in Japan, where the *shogun*—military leader—is ruler. Go carefully. Foreigners may not enter the country and no Japanese may leave.

~ THE ROUTE ~

☞ Follow the *samurai* over the bridge. Japan is divided into three classes, with the *samurai* at the top. *Samurai* wear two swords, are brave and loyal, and have the power to put you to death.

☞ Slip past the *ninja*, waiting at the gate. He is a spy trained to kill enemies.

☞ Turn left. Dart in front of the oxen pulling the *shogun's* wheeled carriage. Most people must travel on foot, or in a carriage called a *kago* carried by men.

☞ Slow down! Poet Matsuo Bashō is working on a poem. His short poems about nature are called *haiku*. In Japanese they have three lines and 17 syllables.

☞ Wander through the houses, past the fan seller to the man flying a kite.

☞ Wave to the woman planting rice in flooded paddies. Rice is like money. It is used to pay taxes.

☞ Turn back and join the young ladies at the pond. Stop and admire the cherry blossoms.

☞ Continue around the pond, slip through the gate, and watch the *samurai* practicing archery. Graceful movements count as much as hitting the bull's-eye!

☞ Follow the white cat and *samurai* into the house for the tea ceremony. Bow as you enter. Drink elegantly. This special event makes you calm and content.

☞ **SEEK THE MAGIC HOURGLASS**
Now it is turquoise.

A RENAISSANCE CITY

You have arrived in Italy at the time of the Renaissance, a period of great learning. This is the prosperous city-state of Florence.

~ THE ROUTE ~

☞ Find artists showing two portraits to wealthy patrons. Patrons help artists by giving them money and telling them what to paint.

☞ Look up at someone about to test a model of Leonardo da Vinci's flying machine. Leonardo is an artist, scientist, and inventor.

☞ Follow the horse and cart carrying sacks of raw fleece through the city to the River Arno. Here it will be washed, spun, woven into cloth, and then dyed. The cloth industry has made the city rich.

☞ Move on to the woman reading a book beside the river. Before the recent German invention of the printing press, books were copied by hand.

☞ Pass the man in green on the bridge. He is jotting down ideas for *The Prince*, a famous book about power and politics. His name is Niccolò Machiavelli.

☞ Run past the pig and on to the musicians. They have been hired by Leonardo da Vinci to make the Mona Lisa smile as he paints her portrait.

☞ Go past the bear on the bridge and find artist Michelangelo. He is working on his statue, *David*, about 16 feet tall.

☞ Join the man standing in front of the domed cathedral. The huge dome was built by architect Brunelleschi, using new and old building techniques.

☞ **SEEK THE MAGIC HOURGLASS**
Now it is white.

EMPIRE OF THE INCAS

You have arrived in South America at Cuzco, capital of the Inca Empire. This vast and powerful empire stretches from Colombia in the north to Chile in the south.

～THE ROUTE～

☞ Find the man entering the city to deliver a duck. He is telling the guard the reason for his visit. Only the Inca nobility, including priests and officials, live in Cuzco.

☞ Meet the official who is tying knots in a string called a *quipu*. He records supplies of food, clothes, weapons, and tools.

☞ Go up some steps to the man carrying a block of stone. The Incas build perfect stone walls without using cement.

☞ Keep going up to the Golden Enclosure of the Sun Temple. Inside is a large image of the sun made of gold.

☞ See the emperor sitting on a pedestal? Approach him backward as a sign of respect. He is said to be descended from the sun god.

☞ Run back down to the man with the block. Turn and pass the runner. He has memorized his message since there is no written language. Relay runners carry messages along the Incas' 15,500 miles of roads.

☞ Hot? Join the man bathing in the clear waters of the river. All the streets are paved, and stone-lined channels bring water and clear away sewage.

☞ Climb onto the bridge and go up the steps to the group of llamas carrying goods. There are no wheeled vehicles, and llamas are the Incas' only pack animals. They are also used for religious sacrifice.

☞ Walk on to the building by the river. It is the emperor's palace. Inside it is richly decorated with silver and precious stones.

☞ **SEEK THE MAGIC HOURGLASS**
Now it is pink.

COLUMBUS IN TROUBLE

It is 1492 and you are on board Christopher Columbus's ship, the *Santa Maria*. Columbus is trying to reach the East Indies from Spain by sailing west around the world. You have been at sea for five weeks and still haven't seen land.

~ THE ROUTE ~

☞ Find the sailor who has joined the crew to avoid going to prison.

☞ Walk toward the front of the ship and watch Columbus trying to calm the crew. They want to go home.

☞ Walk on. Step over sailors sleeping on deck, the only place they can find.

☞ Climb down the ladder to the storeroom, holding your nose. There are no bathrooms on board so both the ship and the crew stink!

☞ Help the steward check the food supplies and then quickly go back on deck.

☞ Climb up to the crow's nest and talk to the sailor on lookout duty. Feel the ship roll.

☞ Go down again. Join the sailor who is looking in the sea for signs of land.

☞ **SEEK THE MAGIC HOURGLASS**
Now it is turquoise.

LAND AHOY! WHERE ARE WE?

You are on board the *Niña*, one of two small ships accompanying Christopher Columbus on his voyage. The other ship is the *Pinta*.

~ THE ROUTE ~

☞ Find the sailor at the water barrel. He is very thirsty, but after five weeks at sea the barrel is empty.

☞ Step across to help the hungry sailor who is fishing.

☞ Cross to the sail maker, mending a sail damaged in a storm.

☞ Swim across to the other ship, the *Pinta*. Watch out for the whale!

☞ Go aboard. Meet Captain Martin Pinzón, who is trying to check the route on a map of the world.

☞ Climb up the mast. Hurrah! The sailor on lookout duty has spotted land.

☞ Climb down quickly, lower the boat, and row toward the shore. Columbus thinks this is the East Indies. In fact it is an island in the Bahamas.

☞ Pass Taino Indians in a canoe. They wonder who you are.

☞ **SEEK THE MAGIC HOURGLASS**
Now it is dark blue.

A COLD AND DRAFTY CASTLE

You are beside the Rhine, a major river that winds through the vast German Empire. The emperor is in power, but princes, nobles, and bishops fight for control of the land. Princes live in castles for safety and to show off their wealth.

~ THE ROUTE ~

☞ Start at the river. Goods are transported along the river by barge because the roads are rough and full of danger.

☞ Follow the road to the castle. Wave to the soldier in the tower. He spies on passing boats, which have to pay a toll for using this stretch of river.

☞ Cross the drawbridge, but don't fall into the moat. Pointed stakes are there to trap you.

☞ Enter the castle and go through to the yard to meet the prince. He is bathing in a tub. It's often warmer outside than inside this cold castle.

☞ Climb the winding stairs and join people at the long table. Sit with your back to the fire, the only place to keep warm. Use hard bread for a plate, and eat with a knife and your fingers.

☞ Feeling sleepy? Follow the cat chasing a mouse upstairs to bed. Draw the curtains for privacy and warmth. Is someone else in the bed? Don't worry. Guests often sleep together!

☞ Now go downstairs again and visit the guard watching the prisoner. Hold your nose. The castle stinks; soon it will get so bad that the prince will have to move away for at least two years.

☞ Look out! Too late! You've fallen through the trapdoor into the dungeon.

☞ **SEEK THE MAGIC HOURGLASS.**
Now it is dark blue.

CITY OF GOLD

You are in Timbuktu in the wealthy empire of Mali. This city south of the Sahara Desert is the center of trade in West Africa.

~ THE ROUTE ~

☞ Find the line of camels carrying salt from the north to be exchanged here for gold from the south.

☞ Follow the goats past the camel park. Sometimes there are as many as 4,000 camels here.

☞ Stop by three men bowing to Mansa Musa, the powerful emperor riding on a camel. He controls the gold, which goes all over the world. Heap ashes on your head as a sign of respect.

☞ Move on to explore the marketplace. People here don't use money. They exchange goods instead.

☞ Step across to the blacksmith under the trees. He is hammering spears for the emperor's large army. Soldiers protect the empire and have made the city safe.

☞ It's time for prayers. Join the two men outside the mosque, the Muslim place of worship. The emperor and many merchants are Muslim.

☞ Hungry? Find the woman who is pounding grain with a long stick. People eat millet, rice, yams, fish, meat, and beans.

☞ Now join the man reading a book in Arabic. Timbuktu is famous as a place of learning.

☞ **SEEK THE MAGIC HOURGLASS**
Now it is brown.

THE ROOF OF THE WORLD

You are high in the Pamir Mountains, hurrying to catch up with Marco Polo on the ancient Silk Road. This is the major trade route between China and the West.

~ THE ROUTE ~

☞ Start at the lake on the left.

☞ Go to the *yurt*, a tent made with goat or camel hair felt. It belongs to nomads, who move from place to place with their animals.

☞ Cross the green fields—some of the best pasture in the world—and run over the log. Beware the brown bear. There are many dangers in these wild mountains.

☞ Find a pile of bones left by wolves. Travelers have put them there to show that you're on the right path.

☞ Hungry? Join the travelers cooking over an open fire. Be patient. At this height, fires burn less brightly and food takes longer to cook.

☞ Go across the log over the stream and stop by the mountain sheep on the other side. Look at his long horns! Shepherds use them to make bowls and fences.

☞ Run ahead to the man playing tunes on a flute. Sing along to keep up your spirits. Ahead lie many bleak and frightening deserts. One is called the Takla Makan. Its name means "if you go in, you'll never come out."

☞ **SEEK THE MAGIC HOURGLASS**
Now it is light blue.

MARCO POLO

You have joined Marco Polo on the ancient Silk Road. He is with travelers carrying gold and precious stones to China.

~ THE ROUTE ~

☞ Join the back of the line of camels.

☞ Meet Marco Polo in the green robe and striped cloak. People have traveled this route for many years but he will be the first European to write about it.

☞ Move ahead to Marco's father carrying a golden tablet. This is a gift from Kublai Khan, ruler of the Mongol Empire, which includes China. It says that the Polos must be given help anywhere in his empire.

☞ Pass Marco's uncle, with a black beard and a long red robe. He is carrying holy oil, a gift to Kublai Khan from the Pope in Italy.

☞ Find two men putting up a signpost to Cathay, their name for China. It's easy to lose your way in the desert.

☞ Quick! Catch the runaway camels. They wear bells to prevent them from getting lost. Camels are ideal for desert travel, as they can go without water for days.

☞ Listen! Can you hear swords clashing? Can you see people fighting in the distance? This is a trick the desert plays on your senses.

☞ Run to the water hole where two camels are resting. Drink up. You won't find water again for hours.

☞ **SEEK THE MAGIC HOURGLASS**
Now it is purple.

A VIKING WINTER

It's winter in Scandinavia, home of the Vikings. These Northmen are mainly farmers, but there isn't enough land for them all. The men are building ships so that when the weather is fair, they can go raiding and trading overseas.

~ THE ROUTE ~

☞ Find the man using a hammer and chisel to carve a rune-stone. Runes are stick-like letters with magical meanings. Rune-stones are set up as monuments to the dead.

☞ Walk past the dog and along the path to the girl milking a cow. Girls learn how to sew and cook, make butter and cheese, spin, weave, ride, swim, and use weapons. When the men are away, the women run the farms.

☞ Continue along the path to the statue of Thor on the right, one of the many gods and goddesses worshipped by the Vikings. Thor is god of thunder and lightning. The day Thursday is named after him.

☞ Run ahead to help the *thralls* collecting firewood on the right. Vikings are divided into three groups, with *thralls*—slaves—at the bottom.

☞ Now wander through the houses and back along the shore to the two boys catching fish. Boys are sometimes sent to live with other families. This helps prevent family feuds.

☞ Step across to the blacksmith, where the *jarl*—leader—is trying on a piece of armor. It is a *byrnie*, a shirt made of thousands of iron rings.

☞ Now lend a hand to the men building oak longships. These ships can travel huge distances at great speed.

☞ Cold and hungry? Go back past the cow and on to the longhouse, where a woman is cooking over an open fire.

☞ **SEEK THE MAGIC HOURGLASS**
Now it is red.

INDIA IN THE RAINS

You have arrived at a village in India, a vast land divided into many states. It is the time of the monsoon, the wind that brings the heavy rains, making the parched earth green and alive.

~ THE ROUTE ~

☞ Find the herdsman guarding the cattle and playing a bamboo flute to keep himself awake. Cattle are a sign of wealth.

☞ Beware the tiger on your left. Villages are fenced to keep out wild animals.

☞ Follow the man with a stick into the village. He is a *brahmin*. Society is divided into four groups or castes, with *brahmins*—priests and men of learning—at the top.

☞ Turn right then left. Can you smell delicious spiced vegetables? This woman is a vegetarian; she believes life is sacred and animals should not be killed for food.

☞ Move on to the holy man sitting on his own. Put some food in his bowl. Holy men are treated with great respect.

☞ Skip past the snake charmer under the trees and stop at the well. Water is precious. It is needed to irrigate the fields during the long dry season after the monsoon.

☞ Pass the cart rumbling through the village and join the people watching the dancers. Each movement of hands, feet, neck, and eyes has a meaning.

☞ Go on to the Hindu temple. Hindus believe all living creatures will live again on earth after they die. Your next life will be a better one if you follow special rules now.

☞ **SEEK THE MAGIC HOURGLASS**
Now it is brown.

A DAY AT THE RACES

You have arrived in Rome, capital of the mighty Roman Empire, which rules over the Western world from Britain to North Africa, and parts of the Middle East. This is the Circus Maximus, the stadium where chariot races are held.

~ THE ROUTE ~

☞ Find the man with a bunch of grapes. He is one of the cheering crowd of 250,000 spectators.

☞ Run down the steps to meet the supporters of the Reds. All drivers belong to one of four teams, which are known by their colors: the Reds, Whites, Greens, and Blues.

☞ Move left to greet the emperor in the royal box. He likes people to come to the races because it makes them happy and this keeps them loyal.

☞ Now join the supporters of the Greens. The front rows are reserved for senators and knights. Everyone comes to the stadium and bets on the races.

☞ Find the Red chariot driven by the champion. Most drivers are slaves, but he has won over a thousand races and is now as rich and famous as a movie star.

☞ Dash across the track to the center of the stadium. It is about 656 feet wide and 1968 feet long. Each race is seven laps.

☞ Quick! Help carry the Blue driver on a stretcher to safety. Drivers have collided and been thrown from their chariots. This is a dangerous sport. Many men and horses are injured on the track.

☞ Join the line of guards in front of the Blues' supporters at the far side of the stadium.

☞ SEEK THE MAGIC HOURGLASS
Now it is red.

SILK AND SECRETS

You have arrived in China, the greatest power in Asia. It is the time of the Han Dynasty, when silk and other luxuries are traded across Asia as far as Rome. This is a wealthy man's house.

~ THE ROUTE ~

☞ Find the horse and carriage in the small courtyard. Look up at the sloping roofs of the house. They are said to keep away evil spirits, which move in straight lines.

☞ Come through the arch and find the boy reading from one of the very first paper scrolls. The Chinese recently invented the art of papermaking.

☞ Say hello to the young woman by the pond with a fan and a silk dress. Do not ask her how silk is made. She could be put to death if she tells you.

☞ Pass the cat and the acrobats. Stop and listen to the musicians. Entertainers often come to the house.

☞ Step across to the man using a brush dipped in ink. He is practicing calligraphy—the art of writing.

☞ Follow the boy with the kite into the kitchen, where cooks are preparing a banquet. There's wild boar and bear's paws, game birds and fish, bamboo shoots and lotus roots.

☞ Hungry? Follow the dog out of the kitchen and enter the house. Kneel on embroidered cushions and eat from small bowls with chopsticks.

☞ **SEEK THE MAGIC HOURGLASS**
Now it is pale orange.

IN THE VALLEY OF THE KINGS

You are in Egypt, the kingdom on the banks of the River Nile. It is 1343 B.C. and this is the funeral of the young king Tutankhamen, who has died at the age of 18 years.

～THE ROUTE～

☞ Help carry the golden throne at the back of the procession. It has been made by skilled craftsmen in the Royal Workshops.

☞ Overtake the golden bed with lion heads. Egyptians believe in life after death so their possessions are buried with them.

☞ Pass the statue of a dog on a box. This is the god Anubis, who will protect the king's body. Egyptians worship many gods.

☞ Move ahead to the golden box on a litter. It contains the king's liver, lungs, stomach, and intestines preserved for his next life.

☞ Walk past the golden statue to the scribe sitting and writing on a papyrus scroll. Egyptians record events using pictures called hieroglyphs.

☞ See the king's body lying on a funeral boat. It has been made into a mummy—prepared with ointments and bandages—to preserve it for thousands of years.

☞ Step forward to meet the king's wife, Ankhesenamen. Only members of the royal family are considered good enough to marry the king. She may also be his niece or even his sister.

☞ Go past the king's model boat and on to the tomb entrance cut into rock. Kings used to be buried in pyramids. Now they are buried deep in the ground where no robber will find them.

☞ **SEEK THE MAGIC HOURGLASS**
Now it is pale orange.

CIRCLE OF STONE

You have arrived in southern Britain during the early Bronze Age. Here people are building Stonehenge, a stone circle that may be used for religious ceremonies and astronomy. It will be built over several centuries.

~ THE ROUTE ~

☞ Find the group of huts. Most people live as farmers and herdsmen. They grow crops and keep herds of animals for food and clothing.

☞ Help pull a sandstone block called a *sarsen*. It weighs over 40 tons and has been dragged 20 miles on rolling logs.

☞ Join the two men in front of the *sarsen*. They keep the logs in line as it moves forward.

☞ Find the four men who are dropping heavy stone balls onto the end of a *sarsen* to shape it. First they weaken the block with fire and water. This stone circle is unusual because the blocks are shaped.

☞ Jump over the deep pit being made ready for a *sarsen*. Borrow a hammer and drive in the stakes.

☞ Help men on timber scaffolding slide a *sarsen* into a pit. Feeling tired? Don't give up. A heavy crosspiece has still to be raised to the top.

☞ Climb up to the man at the top of a *sarsen*. He is shaping knobs that will fit into hollows made in the crosspiece. Skilled craftsmen are needed to build Stonehenge.

☞ **SEEK THE MAGIC HOURGLASS**
Now it is gray.

LORDS OF THE LAND

You are in a forest with the dinosaurs during the Cretaceous period.

~ THE ROUTE ~

☞ Find the nest of duck-billed baby *Corythosaurus*.

☞ Did you hear that crash? Two *Pachycephalosaurus*—"thick-headed lizards"—are butting their heads together.

☞ Pass the *Alamosaurus*, among the last of the giant plant-eating dinosaurs with long necks and small heads.

☞ Step across to two charging dinosaurs with horns. They are *Triceratops*.

☞ Follow the cockroaches down the tree to three ostrichlike dinosaurs—*Ornithomimus*. They can run as fast as racehorses. And they are about to run away now!

☞ Quick! Look up! There's a flurry in the trees and a mighty roar. Can you see that massive head above the trees and the huge curved fangs in its open mouth? It's the dreaded meat-eating *Tyrannosaurus rex*.

☞ See the lizard scamper down the tree. Leap across and hide with it among the first flowering plants in the world.

☞ **SEEK THE MAGIC HOURGLASS**
Now it is gray.

LORDS OF SEA AND SKY

You are swimming through the sun-warm seas of the Cretaceous period. Huge reptiles rule the sea and the sky.

~ THE ROUTE ~

☞ Find ammonites with coiled shells clinging to the rock under the water. These invertebrates—creatures without backbones—are food for the giant sea reptiles.

☞ Meet the *Elasmosaurus*, the reptile with paddles. It is swallowing stones to grind up food in its stomach.

☞ Quick! Dive away from the sharp teeth of the huge, shadowy *Ichthyosaurus*—"fish lizard." Members of its family have swum these waters for millions of years.

☞ Leap out of the water with the *Tylosaurus*—giant sea lizard. It is 30 feet long.

☞ Ride on the back of the giant turtle, *Archelon*. Hold on tight!

☞ Hurry! Look up! *Quetzalcoatlus* are about to swoop for food! With a 40–foot wingspan they are the largest flying creatures ever.

☞ Climb out of the water. Dash along the shore and run for the safety of the hills.

☞ **SEEK THE MAGIC HOURGLASS**

Now it is light blue.

Slurp!

Out of my way!

Swim faster!